Achievers Handbook 2

(Over 100 Inspirational Keys to fulfill your Destiny)

Achievers Best Guide Series Book Two

IKECHUKWU JOSEPH

Copyright © 2024 Ikechukwu Joseph
All rights reserved.
ISBN: 9798346485889

DEDICATION

to all aspiring high achievers.

CONTENTS

1	Positioning and repositioning yourself for strategic achievements (Nuggets 1-10).	Pg1
2	Awake the Champion in you (Nuggets 11-20).	Pg5
3	Learn from the Masters, our heroes past (Nuggets 21-30).	Pg8
4	About Potentials: decode, discern, determine and decide (Nuggets 31-40).	Pg11
5	You can be what you want to be (Nuggets 41-50)	14
6	Reevaluate yourself, Realign your tools, Readjust and Reengineer your Plans (Nuggets 51-60).	Pg17
7	Work and fit the broken Pieces (Nuggets 61-70)	Pg20
8	Apply the right Plugins (Nuggets 71-80)	Pg23
9	Seizing the right Opportunities (Nuggets 81-90)	Pg26
10	Leisure time is necessary and medicinal (Nuggets 91-103)	Pg29

Appreciation	Pg 32
Appendix A	Pg 33
Appendix B	Pg 35
About the Author	Pg 41
Author's Contact	Pg 42

1 POSITIONING AND REPOSITIONING YOURSELF FOR STRATEGIC ACHIEVEMENTS

Nugget No.1 - Anointing (God's element in you) provokes the essentials of your potentials and destroys the negative yoke of your potentials.

- Anointing is the crowning and fortifying presence of God in your life and in what you do whether a business man or a preacher. It is the lubricant to oil your wheel, the facilitator, the enabler that encourages you when the chips are down and you are tired and want to quit. It is that still small voice you hear as God urging you to move on, you can do it, you can win and you can overcome. Always start with God if you want to get God's outstanding results.

Nugget No.2 - Positioning and repositioning yourself for strategic achievements.

- Someone said that if you change your position God will change your situation. Adjustments are what makes the sweets and bitters of life go round. Appropriate additions and subtractions are inputs to life processes that create equitable balance. Zacchaeus was desperate to see Jesus but the crowd barred him as he was short in height. What did he do? He repositioned himself by climbing up the tree above everyone else - knowing what to do in times like this. Your position determines how far you can see and what freedom you have to access in life.

Nugget *No.3 - You can turn your Frightful frustration into fortifying fortunes*

- How? Employ courage, to stand up to problems. Courage is a weapon. Courage is bravery in the face of danger, audacity to confront, daring where others fail, nerve and resolution in indecision. First, separate the fright from the frustration so you can deal with them separately and adequately. Fear is a killer. He robes and stripes you naked before he kills. If you must fear then fear your own fears and fearfully respect God. Don't fear the weather, your circumstances, and the enormousness of the problem. Convert your fears to fortune

Nugget No 4 - Humble attitudes can take you to high altitudes

- Humble yourself before God and he will exalt you in due season. Pride they say goes before a fall. Humility makes for diligence and if you see a man diligent in his pursuit he will stand before great men and kings. Arrogance is provocative and no one wants to align with an arrogant fellow no matter how savvy he may be. Humble attitudes breed straight thinking, determination and focus.

Nugget No.5 - You can turn your impeaching importunity into optimal Opportunities

- Opportunities are all around you to discover. They are in problems you face that are to be solved. They are in your environments as projects to execute, in your mind as clues and ideas to invest in and even in failures of others if you can see what they did not see or do what they did not do right. But be careful about opportunities that take you away from God. Importunity brings out the ruggedness in you, the shameless persistence and persevering insistence and supplication that eventually bring you succor.

Nugget No.6 - In life if you waste time, time will in turn waste you.

- Time has a life span. The time you wasted yesterday is what you are suffering today. Time and seasons are linked to opportunities. If one season escapes you then don't let the next. Every day we meet opportunities – use them. **Procrastination they say is a lazy man's apology.** Wake up from your slumber and start shooting.

Nugget No.7 - Your credentials are proof producers

- Show me your work and I will present and access your credentials. Your credentials are just beyond the credits and alphas your papers present. They are your worth – the values you have made out of life's issues. Credentials are evidential and credible records you produce written and unwritten as a proof of your worth.

- You must then strife with all your might to be something so you can be somebody. Get education, more education, more skills, technical know-how, better attitude and aptitude. You are born to win and you have everything that you need to succeed. Ride on friend.

Nugget No.8 - Your credentials are identifiers, mark pointers that provide and points to visual directions.

- If you have one then your focus in life is evident. It only tells you where to concentrate your energies, thoughts, and finances. You cannot be jack of all trade. Whatever your calling in life, you should improve yourself on that line. If your calling came at birth first like David then add education to validate it and if education first then add the right attitudes and skills to regularize it. Where are your credentials pointing you to? Then look up to God the enabler, to yourself esteem then to your environment for resources and launch out to rule your world.

Nugget No.9 – Doing something good the wrong way will always keep the doors closed. Sow a viable seed on good ground

- Manuals, handbooks and reference books like Achievers Best Guide series are meant to help. To inspire and be consulted in times of confusion or need so all other self-help books. Why then doing thing the ways that they ought not to be done? Are you a magician? No wonder you are failing and receive no reward for your hard work, working in the wrong directions. Ask the experts if you need to. We are meant to complement each other

Nugget No.10 - Don't focus on your inadequacies but on your abilities and strengths. Forget tomorrow at the moment and concentrate on today

- There is something good in you even when you and others do not see it. God created you in his own very image and likeness. Who then told you that you are no good or a dummy? That is why you should discover who you are, the real you the way God intended you to be and what he created you to fulfill in life. Then focus to achieve those goals you have drawn from Gods plan for your life. Position and reposition yourself to excel.

2 AWAKE THE CHAMPION IN YOU

Nugget No.11 - Your failure today must not determine your future. .Learn to forgive your past mistakes and move ahead

- What did you learn from what befell you - the failure, the loss, the shortage and the mistakes. What lessons you learned are the clues to the solution that will see you through at the next attempt. Champions were not made champions over nights. They went from lighter and feather weights to heavy weights, from amateur to mature, from toddlers to top scorers, and from kids to kings.

Nugget No.12 - Awake the champion in you

- Mediocrity will never make masters. There are sleeping giants inside you that are supposed to be Generals in warfronts, giant technocrats, orators, speakers, singers, captains of industries. The world is waiting for you. Don't die a mediocre and unfulfilled.

Nugget No.13 - Saul they sang killed a thousand (qualified Success) but David killed ten thousands (qualified, quantified and certified Success).

- It is good to finish with a result, good result, qualified and certified results and outcome. There is joy in victory so always aim at the highest. **The king in the kid David won where the king in Saul failed. Boldness is not in size or loudness but in** inner strength.

Nugget No.14 - There's sweet healing forgiveness in learning to forget your past failures so as to heal your tomorrow.

- It will help you embrace and face the future with great confidence, hope and expectations. Those who run a race prepare, concentrate and avoid distractions if they must win. There are lots of distractions around you enough to sway you but move ahead because what matters is a successful end and not the rough means to the end.

Nugget No.15 - Grow your inner man.

- Strength is not physical but spiritual. Make time for meditation and prayers for the soul grows lean in activities and unfruitful ventures. Grow your soul to go, grow and glow. Sharing with others, learning from others and listening to those who know what you don't know will help out if you are humble enough to learn at the feet of your seniors or the masters.

Nugget No.16 - Be quiet in and out and let God speak to you.

- His voice will come to you inside as business ideas, inspirations, clues, solutions and answers and heard in your waiting heart. Speak for the servant hears. Be still and know that I am your God who conceals for you to discover and I am God that reveal secrets to those who seek my face. Receive insight, great discoveries in your life and endeavors in Jesus name.

Nugget No.17 - They say readers are leaders or leaders are readers too.

- Leaders are readers of manuals of life, handbooks to draw inspirations from, guidebooks so they don't stumble and reference books when they forget so they do not deceive the people. They learn from the past heroes and heroines – their failures so they do not fail like them, their mistakes so they be cautious to deliver what will win the trust of their subjects. Champions are made and their feat never inherited or passed on.

- Read and read to enrich your think tank and have references to fall back on in times of need. Find resources in reading. They say readers are leaders or leaders are readers too

Nugget No.18 - This charge I commit unto you Timothy my son war a good warfare

- This same advice I humbly give unto you in your endeavors and career play safe, fair and sane because what you sow you will also reap. Strive lawfully and legitimacy will crown your endeavors. Things got through the rims of the plate swiftly go the same way.

Nugget No.19 - You can create sense out of nonsense. You can create something out of nothing. You can create wealth out of dearth.

- How? For the non-sense situation remove or subtract the non that made it insane and it will be sane. For the nothing replace the no- with some- and you have something. Analyzing and dissecting your problem gives insight on what to do. You can create wealth out of austere inflation and scarcity by applying the right financial formulae.

Nugget No.20 - Every problem has a cause, a course and a consequence.

- To resolve the problem - find the cause and follow the course, roadmap for the solution and pattern of the course to find a solution. Every cause has an effect (identify and remedy it). Every effect has a consequence (gives feedback for further action) and every consequence has absolutions or solutions (Results). Champions solve problems by winning contests, battles and resolving puzzles to become champions.

3 LEARN FROM THE MASTERS, OUR HEROES PAST

Nugget No.21 - Follow and learn from the Masters

- Those who know more than you, who have more than you have in your field of endeavor because they have seen it all before your arrival. Paul lived what he preached and preached what he lived so he enjoins us to learn from the masters of the craft we follow.

Phil. 4:9

Those things which you have both learned and received and heard and seen in me do and the God of peace shall be with you.

Nugget No.22 - Familiarity with the secret place is familiarity with the glory place. Abide in his presence.

- Prayers in season and out of season, defensive and offensive prayers, petitions and supplications and various types of prayers will help keep you in the presence of God where your provisions and protection is guaranteed. You need His grace to attain His glory. We need God's grace in our race in life.

Nugget No.23 -.Discover, uncover and recover all

- Discover what you want to do, uncover involvements financially or physically and go to work, invest and recover all your lost glory and succeed.

Nugget No.24 - Learning to live in the Spirit of prayers hour by hour decorates your life with insights, revelations, visions and blessings .

– Learn how and where ideas come from, in the silence of your mind and meditative mode of your actions and reactions in life's struggle. Prayers mentally will supply your minds with relevant issues but spiritually will make you see through. See the truth.

Nugget No.25 - Ignorance, the bane of the ignoramus

- God abhors ignorance .It destroys (Hosea 4:6). Ignorance kept the impotent man in the waiting list for thirty eight years. What you do not know, you do not know but can know if you try. No ignorant person has ever succeeded in the process or project they are ignorant or ill-informed of.

Nugget No.26 - Every call, vocation, profession, or career need the right tools to succeed

They need an open door of utterance, inspiration, faith and will to succeed. Utterance comes from God and is revelation knowledge. They need *"Rhema,"* where a speaker unveils the truth and different listeners receive insights differently and severally from the same source to the solutions of their multifarious problems. Your career needs inspirational encouragement, intimate convincing faith, assurance strong and self-will to succeed in your pursuit. What are your callings?

Nugget No.27 – Stop, look, listen before you leap

- Stop, that is waiting on God, then looking inward (reassess and reexamine), Listen (prepare, readjust) before you leap (invest).

- Be careful, check, reassess before you make a commitment, before you agree, before put your seal and signature to what will bind you all your life or career.

Nugget No.28 - The provisions you need to fulfill you ministry or mission is locked up in the open doors of utterance, faith and the call.

- So pursue your career and you will unlock the truths of the process, the reasons of the choice you made, the resources you need to break even along the line or rather the journey. The beginning might be bleak and bitter, midway discouraging but the end of the tunnel will show the light. Start with the not enough you have and do not forget the days of little beginnings until you get to more than enough. Grow your capital from micro to mega, be judicious, thoughtful and you will add more.

Nugget No.29 - In discovery therapy you ask life's questions and you find the answers

- Ask factual, probing, analytical, pragmatic and technical questions and attempt to proffer logical answers. Get into inquiry and discovery process and uncover the nitty-gritty of your project or problems so you can recover the solution

Nugget No.30 - The difference between the ordinary and extraordinary is the extra.

- Go the extra mile and enter your extraordinary success. If you add an extra to the ordinary you get the extra ordinary. If you want to be great then attempt great things. **Great people are only ordinary people who attempted great runs and attained great feats and achievements.**

4 ABOUT POTENTIALS - DECODE, DISCERN, DETERMINE AND DECIDE

Nugget No.31 - During your waiting time look inward to yourself, upward to God, then outward to your environment

- Your waiting time is like the gestation period. It is a junction in life you are about to make a great decision that will affect your whole life and future – a career to pursue, a course to study, a wife or husband to marry, a project to invest in and a path to follow in life. Look inward you to you capacity and capability, then upward to the God of providence and then outward to friends, relations and associates, government and non-governmental bodies for all the help you can get.

Nugget No.32 - Utterance we say comes from God but must be prayed up.

- Divine utterances are pregnant with answers but must be delivered and accessed to meet a need. The place of prayers breeds the presence of God. Utterance from God comes to those listening in his presence.

Ps. 91:1

He that dwelleth in the secret place of the most high shall abide under the shadow of the almighty

Nugget No.33 - God never gave an empty promised land to

Israel but one full of oppositions and giant enemies.

- With the milk and honey flowing in the Promised Land were the Canaanites, Hittites, Amorites, Jebusites and so on contesting for the same promise and provision. That means there is work to do to enter your promised land. Poverty only steers in the face of those who fold their hands and sleep. Arise oh sleeper for the night is far gone and the morning is here. Hunger is waiting at the door of the Lazy man

Nugget No.34 - Meeting people and making them relevant to yourself and your needs.

- You need the Moses that will bring you out of oddity, oblivion and the Joshua to follow up, the David to intervene or bail you out in time of distress. No one is an Island neither a have it or know it all. So you need people, relevant people and even the irrelevant that will put you on your toes and cause crises if you only know crisis management.

Nugget No.35 - Excluding the God of providence in your life's configuration and design is like removing the thermostat from a thermodynamic system .

- You need balance for optimal and maximal output. You need God your reference and consultant.

Nugget No.36 – Do, be, live and achieve

- Doing is the beginning of being. Being is the beginning of living and living is the essence of achieving and achieving is the spices of life. So do, so that you be and live to achieve

Nugget No.37 - The discipline of doing will keep you ahead.

- Do not let the kid factor in you kill the king factor in you. The angle you tilt to will express your brand and you, Discipline, self-control or restraint are virtues that will bring out the king in you. Learn from David when it mattered most the king in his kid statues arose and defeated Goliath. Work while you may for the night comes when no one will work. You are not growing any younger. Do, do and do till you get it right.

Nugget No.38 - For every man-made built in failure, there is a

God-made built in Grace to the rescue

- His grace is always sufficient for you. That you were born with that problem does not mean you have to live with it. Your might and ability will fail you because it is not by might nor power but by his Spirit says the Lord. Depend on God

Nugget No.39 - Lift your eyes and look on the fields (John 4:35).

- There are viable ventures and opportunities. It is harvest time. What are you waiting for? Open your eyes and see gold where others see stones. See hope where others see hopelessness and see a future where they say there is no future. The young must grow.

Nugget No.40 - Grace is described as Gods riches at Jesus expense .

- Avail yourself of grace, grace infinite grace on the cross of Calvary where he said it is finished. He paid the price for your freedom to God's riches. Enter into your rest.

5 YOU CAN BE WHAT YOU WANT TO BE

Nugget No.41 - Locate Gods place for you. It is a place of Gold

- The secret place: of the almighty will help (psalm 91:1). The secret place is the presence of God. It is the place of prayers, private communion with you and your God. The only secrecy here is because your communion with God who sees your private life and heartache in secret will reward you in secret. There is nothing secret about it. This place is very important in the course of your discovering and recovering Divine secrets are hidden truths of the plan and purpose of God about a thing, a place or your life. Locate the will of God for your life and remain with it if you want to succeed in life. God so trusted Abraham that he shared his plans with him about Sodom and Gomorrah (Gen 18:17). They that wait upon the Lord shall renew their strength; they will uncover the secret of strength with God. God's secrets are confidential plans, hidden treasures, mysteries, game plans or counsels

Nugget No.42 - You can be what you want to be.

- The sky they say is your limit but I dare say that the sky can be your starting point because with God there is no limit. God's resources and riches are unlimited for you to explore. Put your will in the will of God and take a flight into an adventure and rule your world. What do you want to be? An engineer, astronaut, accountant or what? The world is big enough to accommodate you and the desires of your inner heart. With God nothing shall be impossible. **You can can if you can just can or try out**

Nugget No.43 - Act out your faith in the inside (inside faith - attitude) and act out your faith on the outside (outside faith - action) to attain equilibrium for equitable result

- Faith work is all about action inside out. Faith without works they say is a dead faith. Show me your work and I will show you my commensurate faith. It is not enough to call God all day without acting out your faith. Faith and work go together. **When you work add faith and when you faith add commensurate work to get result**

Nugget No.44 - For your potentials uncover and find out your "influentials."

- Find out the people, the places, the resources, the associations, the education or the problems that will affect the course and consequences of your choice, career, profession or ministry. You need to access them for better understanding and know how to integrate.

Nugget No.45 - 'My heart's burden for you is that you

Never ever abort or scuttle a divine plan because of impatience and ignorance

- That will mean another Mary-go-round. How many people are living wasted lives today or how many people are living unfulfilled lives today because they are yet to find the place of God in their lives? How many people are jack of all trades doing this and that without finding fulfillment?

His hands are touching me

His words are transforming me

His heart is loving me

Nugget No.46 - Love is sharing. Your life and business has a love angle too.

- When God blesses you, stretch out your hands to others. **Share the blessings as well as your tears. What you share is shared and borne with your listeners**

Nugget No.47 - To uncover you must look for vestiges, traces of evidence, bloodline, your roots, foundations or ancestral landmarks

- Landmarks, relics or history about your foundations are markers to note in your journey in life because they have or will have contributions, positive or negative to make for your success or failure. To excel you must deal with them accordingly.

Nugget No.48 - Divine access depends on locating, identifying God's codes or numbers

- God is accessible and available. God delights in his people and word. God is his word and his word is God. So what button will you press in the word of God to cue or log into his riches.

Nugget No.49 - Dynamics of Faith - how faith works

- The faith-word (faith in the word), the faith action (faith in your actions), faith belief (faith in believing), and faith confessions (positive confession) are needed in your daily living. Your faith must be tried or tested before the triumphs.

Nugget No.50 - After the effervescence at the top, the water settles at the bottom. After the boiling at the top then comes the cooling down at the bottom .

- The proverbial bed bug told the children to be calm because with time every hot thing will get cold. You are not at the end of the world yet, so do not end it. Keep on shooting marksman until you are done with victory. It is only enough when you feel the joy of victory.

6 REEVALUATE YOURSELF, REALIGN YOUR TOOLS, READJUST AND REENGINEER YOUR PLANS

Nugget No.51 - Prove your faith in the valley not just on the mountaintop

- It is not easy to say it is well when you are inside the well. When things are tough it is only the tough that keeps going. You can prove your faith in hard times and do not chicken out when problems come. Problems should test and strengthen our faith. Fight the good fight of faith.

Nugget No.52 - Reevaluate yourself, realign your tools, readjust and reengineer your plans

- Periodically check and assess yourself and work – am I doing it right? Check and balances! Realign your tools, instruments of operations where necessary. Rearrange and tinker your plans in line with the realities of times and situations

Nugget No.53 - Daniel denied his flesh of food and the king's merriment for 21 days just to provoke the presence/and visitation of God

- Sacrifice! If you want to succeed in life you must make sacrifices by denying yourself certain temporary sweets for the purposes of advancing your course. Sometimes withdrawal from public glare, from things that have temporary value so you can gain greater and permanent spiritual and physical values is necessary.

Nugget No.54 - Every seed carries a potential Tree.

- No seed no harvest, no sowing no reaping, if you talk of harvest it is because there was sowing and seed time. Seed is your investment or project. Prepare and provide for tomorrow by investing in today.

Nugget No.55 - Taking the land, entering your rest involves dealing with the gates that locked out the people and the cities

- Gates and spiritual gates in particular must be dealt with if you must possess your possessions. May be you have done all stipulated in handbook one and no success yet. Deal with your spiritual gates that tend to obstruct your progress. The spiritual they say control the physical. Deal with the spiritual adequately; dismantling spiritual gates, breaking evil covenants and curses in prayers and you will make way for physical development. Prayers, prevailing prayers will avail and give you leverage.

Proverbs 11:8

The righteous is delivered out of trouble, and the wicked cometh in his stead.

Nugget No.56 - A team is better because it is a collection of aptitudes and attitudes multiplied.

- Two good heads they are better than one. Team work with well-coordinated leadership will accelerate your progress. Let your work force work in groups and smaller unit especially policy makers. Board room meetings, management meeting and stake holders meetings will improve your work force and organizations. Dare to form and work in teams and see rapid progress and increased output.

Nugget No.57 - You are alive because there is something to live for

- We can walk on the sea, be safe in the storm and calm in the fire if we know and have inner information or revelation knowledge of why we were created in the first place. You are on earth for a purpose so endure and if possible enjoy the ride while your time last. The determinant factor in life is determination. Willpower, fortitude and courage are survival formula elements. **Some people barely live; some rarely survive while others merely exist**

Nugget No.58 - While we are looking up to heaven for God to respond, God is looking down to the earth for someone to act.

- God expects us to act out our faith on the promises of God, be strong and do exploit, to rule and reign in life. While we are looking up to heaven for God to come down, God is looking down to earth for someone to come up, to storm the heavens in prayers

Nugget No.59 - In spiritual warfare we win our physical battles.

- What do you do when you are confronted with obstacles impinging on and interfering with your work or contract or oppositions from your colleagues or direct boss, when your faith is threatened and compromise looms. **This is time to kneel your way to triumph, bind all the "bindables," untie all the "untieables" and loosen all the "loosables."**

Nugget No.60 - Sowing is an investment, an input, and the ability to commit, surrender, and deposit a seed, into the ground expecting to reap.

- Sow a viable seed in a good soil today if you want to reap good yield tomorrow. Invest in someone's life, in a worthwhile project or in genuine Gods work. That is hope come alive. A worthwhile investment today will eventually worth your while.

7 WORK AND FIT THE BROKEN PIECES

Nugget No.61 - I know your works, I have set before you an open door and none can shut it

- Reward for a case of faithfulness. It is the case of Philadelphia church. Hard work pays but hard work and smart work with right handiwork and aptitude pays better. What is the worth of your work? People work but what value will your hard work generate. Everyone's work will be tried, analyzed, assessed and valued by assessment fire. Therefore let your product be profitable and not worthless.

Nugget No.62 - Disappointments are part of life processes.

- Don't worry about all those who left when you needed them most. All that left you (stranded) were not meant to stay. All who stayed were meant for you for the time being – friends, workers, associates or confidants. Every disappointment they say is a blessing because it gives room to look elsewhere. Any available option or diverse options to choose from, makes for better evaluation.

Nugget No.63 - Don't wait to get everything before you do anything.

- Do anything feasible you can towards getting everything you aspire to. You may not get everything you need, recipes, money, or time etc. at once. Getting one option and the next available option at a time will set the pace for the next task in fixing the broken pieces or puzzles facing you.

Nugget No.64 - Work with the broken pieces.

- If you can fit and fix your dream project together then the picture of what next or the remains will become clearer and the springboard for the next task. Those pieces or ashes or relics are strong links between the available observables and the expected, between the past and present, between the starter and finisher and between your goal and the gold. Never stop working until you work it out.

Nugget No.65 - In your invisible secret storms, God is your present help.

- Hold on to the forte. You may have been torn apart, tossed up and down that you strength can no longer bear to hold. He is there with you in trouble and has always been there. Only that you did not notice. Draw courage from the one that promised that he will never leave you nor forsake you. Open up and you will be amazed at help waiting for you and your career or projects. **Secrecy may be sacred but do not carry any secrete to your grave that is meant to be revealed to help the world. Secrete storms that has no vent may tear you apart.**

Nugget No.66 - Learning to be silent, to be still before God, allows us to listen and hear.

- Hearing is the precursor to doing as listening is to hearing. A lot of mistakes today are the result of not listening, hearing or deafness. Deafness is a result of malfunctioning auditory structures or stubbornness. We need to hear the voice of God in our inner being to survive the struggles of life. Stop, look and listen especially to God and some say to your heart before you take action.

Nugget No.67 - Spiritual giants or business moguls are only willing, available and thirsty babies who paid the price for the prize

- Tycoons, business magnates, entrepreneurs, industrialists or experts never came from the moon but were small men who breathed same air like any other. The only difference was that they were determined, willing and available to pay whatever price to attain their goal and get the gold. To fulfill your destiny be willing, available and thirsty for success. **It is not enough to show interest but you must be seen to do interest.**

Nugget No.68 – Mental thinking prayers will supply your mind's faculties with relevant ideas but spiritual physical prayers will see you through.

- See the truth and pursue the truth to a logical conclusion. Pray up the inspirational keys and then pray through to unlocking your potentials and closed doors. **Use not only your heart but your head also in life's pursuit.** Do not forget the good ways your mother taught you about God's mysterious ways. Many great singers, scientists, orators and those who have made it in life the world over started and learned their acts and arts from the church which most of them have deserted today becoming anathema. Go back to your roots, to the God of heaven whom your Fathers served.

Nugget No.69 - Strategic spiritual warfare is a tactical war you fight in the spirit with your spiritual man against spiritual opposition to address physical problems.

- You need wisdom that stems from knowledge (information) and understanding (analyzed information) to address your problems both physically and spiritually. The world is a battle field where wars are won and lost. It is also a stage where everyone displays your accolades and go to render accounts. (For more see "Strategic Spiritual Warfare" by Ikechukwu Joseph).

Nugget No.70 - There is a link between the blessings of God in your life and His purpose in you

- Whatever you receive from God as blessings have a link to what he wants you to do. God wants you to be a source of blessings too to others. He never blessed you to go on riotous living or jamboree like the prodigal son. Find the link to sustain the flow and fulfill the purpose of your life. Live a purposeful life – purposeful career, purposeful marriage, purposeful relationship etc.

8 APPLYING THE RIGHT PLUGINS

Nugget No.71 - When your life style plugins fit God's purpose in your life, success follows.

- Applying the right plugins – I mean appendages, additions, extensions, tools you acquire and add to your life and work to help you fulfill your dreams in life. Let your purpose be the purpose of God too. Do not use plugins that will destroy what you want to achieve eventually. Watch what you take in as the system will only give back what it has taken in. Garbage in, garbage out!

Nugget No.72 - The spirit of man (spirit man) receives from God directly and the soul receives from the word of God (transformation, faith, courage)

- Train your spirit (small letter) to listen as is the contact to God through God's Spirit (capital letter) so it can receive information or revelation knowledge. Then applying the right knowledge from a renewed soul leads to a transformed life and success. Remember that the Spirit (capital letter) bears witness with our own spirit (small letter) that we are the children of God.

Nugget No.73 - A seed sown has a potential fruitful tree inside it.

- Sow the right seed into the right soil and at the right season then wait and watch expectantly for the harvest. Your wait and watch period is when you plug in all the loopholes and tie all the loose ends, pruning, trimming, tending and nurturing your vine yard. The seed you sow is your investment, your business capital, contributions, give-away and even gifts.

Nugget No.74 - Success therapy: discover, uncover and recover all.

- In discovery you identify the problems, the issues. In uncovering you analyze and dissect what you identified as the problem to find out the nitty-gritty. Then in recovery you proffer the antidote, remedy and corrective measures to earn success (for more see my book, Discover, Uncover and Recover all - the Ziklag Experience by Ikechukwu Joseph).

Nugget No.75 - Peter put them all out and knelt down and prayed.

- Delete your excess luggage and give God space. In desperate situations you need to do the needful, avoiding all even the good but needless at point in time. Peter knew what to do in needful situations. He knew that prayer was and is still the key. Prayers and lots of bended knees are powerful plugins that can save you lots of embarrassment and shame.

Nugget No.76 - God is available and accessible in your thinking, impulses and impressions on your mind, so login

- Do not ask or wonder where God is in times of distress. He is there with you and has been there all along only you never put more effort to notice and draw inspirations. God is available and accessible. All the tools and provisions you need are available so sign up in repentance if you are a new user and log in if you are a returning user.

Nugget No.77 - Your call has a purpose, a pursuit, vision, commission and honor.

- So whatever is your calling or profession in life, identify and focus on the purpose, embark on the pursuit, stay with the vision and commission so that at last you can earn laurels.

Nugget No.78 - When we pray God gives us the worth of what we asked for.

-He gave Sarah and not Eve to Abraham because if Abraham is the Father of all nations he will need a mother for all nations. God promised a wife meet (suitable) not mate. God gives us our needs (needful and necessary) and not our wants. **Money may attract the woman you want, but prayer attracts the woman you need.** God is concerned with the worth of what we have or pursue. Does it have any eternal and spiritual value or just mundane earthily sensual quality? **Do you eat to live or just live to eat? What kind of life are you living?**

Nugget No.79 - Intense burning desire inside you is the clue to what God wants you to do if you are in communion with Him.

- Interest, intense hunger, peace of mind after making a decision might be clues to the direction God is pointing you to. God speaks to us differently so you must discover how God is to you. Is it inner witness, strong impressions, dreams, or insight? **Insight sees how (solution) but the eyes see what (result or outcome).**

Nugget No.80 - Thoughts, intentions or feelings cannot comprehend God but they can see and acknowledge the works of God

- So see God with your spiritual eyes to understand and with the physical eyes to acknowledge and appreciate Him. Always inquire of the Lord like the prophets of old whenever you do not understand. Clearance, better understanding will save us a lot of, had I known and mistakes which are retrogressive.

9 SEIZING THE RIGHT OPPORTUNITIES

Nugget No.81- Grace is described as Gods riches at Jesus expense.

- His grace is sufficient for you. Grace is unmerited and undeserved favor so avail yourself of this gesture. There are times in this life when we just receive the mercy and grace of God. You got the job when there were more qualified candidates. Why is it not you involved in that accident? Why are you the one celebrated when more skilled ones were there before you and by no act of yours you got the slot and by their own act they lost to you. Is God partial? No, God has designed the times and seasons in his own will.

Nugget No.82 – Opportunity, the barren Shunamite woman shared in solving Elisha's food and accommodation problems and got God's reward of a child

- She cashed in on the opportunity of helping out to receive God's blessings. She had been childless and this kind gesture of hers brought and bought her a child. Will you see and recognize an opportunity when one comes your way? Every day and everywhere opportunities abound but elude us because we fail to see them. Find them in problems that need solutions, in needs of your communities. When there is scarcity of water then this is an opportunity to sink a bore hole and provide water at a cost. When no health facilities or in times of epidemic, a hospital, when no school or market you build a shopping center or recreational facilities and make money. Open your eyes now, look out for and seize opportunities.

Nugget No.83 - making the very most use of the time (buying up each opportunity) because the days are evil Eph. 5:16

- Use time when it is available to you. You may have the raining season, which is time to farm for you cannot do that when the season is over. So you have seasonal fruits. There is time for everything under the sun - time opportunity. There are opportunities that come with season time, age time, day time or night times.

Nugget No.84 – Do not let your God-given ideas, talents, impressions, inner vision, dreams or thought die inside you

- Let it out and share it with friends, parents, sponsors and people or organizations that will be of use to your dreams. Avoid destiny killers or people who will steal your ideas without giving you the credits. For example if you have a manuscript registers the copyright first. Get patent rights, license for your products or work. There are legal rights you own or laws that protect your intellectual works (books, songs, music, inventions or discoveries).

Nugget No.85 - Therefore, as we have opportunity, let us do good to all people, especially to those who belong to the household of faith (Gal. 6:10)

- Seizing the right opportunities when they come your way. Not opportunities to exploit and cheat others but to help. When you do that the benefits return to you. When you seize the right opportunities the right returns, profit, yield and proceeds come to you. Doing good is like sowing a seed and you never know which seed will germinate and make your day. **The Bible says that he that scatter (cheerful and generous giver) reaps back but he that withholds (miser, stingy, closefisted) comes to poverty**

Nugget No.86 - We were created equally but differently. We complement each other.

- Partnership: Discover not only Gods deposit in you – the gem, gold, talents, nuggets, pearls, expertise or experience but also people that can complement, enhance or supplement your efforts. We need partners in life just like in marriage of the husband and wife. I do not mean purposeless marriages or partnerships. Get marriage of ideas, of expertise, of experience and strength or of adulthood and youthfulness. Get the other part of you that until now has left you and your work incomplete and unfulfilled. For example the medical doctor needs a nurse or laboratory technologist and even a clerk or messenger.

Nugget No.87 - Every problem has one immediate cause, many remote causes, long term and short term effects

- The immediate cause is the one you see, the last straw that broke the Carmel's back and may be linked to several other remote causes way behind. For example in an accident, careless driving may be the immediate cause but behind this careless driving may be anger from a previous quarrel, absent mindedness because of a family problem or the person had a nervous or narcotic problem. So you have to diagnose correctly and proffer solution.

Nugget No.88 - Optical or visual illusion and deception.

- Does an open eye mean an open vision? "Mind the glass," caution sign have saved a lot of people from crashing into a separating glass even with their eyes widely open. Don't be deceived by what you see. You may be mistaken. Are you color blind then seek help. Watch the road signs and signs of the times for a guide and guard. You need all the signs to time you into the correct target.

Nugget No.89 - When last did you hear from God?

- No wonder everything turned out sour after all the hard work. We need God's guide and guard because he knows our future. God knows when the sun will be up, when the waves will be turbulent and the winds contrary. It will be far better if we can predict correctly the rise and fall of the market.

Nugget No.90 - Marketing consists of creating relationships

- To sell yourself or products, goods and services you need to meet and relate with the right people. You need a platform to showcase yourself. You need a website and internet presence to reach the world. You need social media and technology to access your market. What you are reading now is made possible because of sharing my knowledge through modern technology and internet. Relate with people and your environment.

10 LEISURE TIME IS NECESSARY AND MEDICINAL

Nugget No.91 - Heaven is still above and the earth is still beneath. The flow is still from top to bottom.

- Try as much as possible to keep alive if you must get to the top where it matters. Enough rest will give you enough strength. You are still human with potentials to be strong and weak so tread softly. Slow and steady they say win the race.

Nugget No.92 - Make time for meditation and prayers as the soul grows lean in activities. Grow your soul to glow"

- Planning will save you a lot of worry and anxiety. Plan your time to include rest as well as other essential things. Too much activity wearies the soul and weakens the body. Have time to meditate and talk issues over with your God. A healthy mind will make a great thinker. Thinkers tinker through life.

Nugget No.93 Do you know that 60% alkalinity and 40% acidity balance in your diet is good for you.

- Watch what you eat for they are part of you thought, physiological, biochemical and working processes. Periodically check your doctor for medical advice about your health and nutrition. Eat well to stay health. Any healthy man is ready to go. Balanced diet is the answer to your nutritional needs.

Nugget No.94 - There's sweet healing forgiveness, in learning to forget the past.

- It will help you embrace and face the future. Silence all the negative voices and weights that drag you down. You were not the first and neither will you be the last. The good thing is that you have come out of it. Your failure today or yesterday must not determine your tomorrow. Learn to forgive your past mistakes and move ahead.

Nugget No.95 - Don't focus on your inadequacies but on your abilities and strengths. Forget tomorrow and concentrate on today

- As long as you are living you have strength and abilities. This should be your area of primary assignment. Work on it to improve your capabilities. Polish your potentials to produce the shine that will attract attention. Start with what you can do to what you cannot, from what you have to what you do not have, from where you are to where you want to go. Even your inadequacies can be converted to strength. For how see my book, "Discovering Yourself."

Nugget No.96 - Learn to say it is well even when you are inside the well

- Hope is the answer to survival in rough environments you were called to work. Ask the miner when the gold or diamonds is in his hands. Hope that brings courage will keep your oil burning and your light shining. The coward dies many times before his death. I say may your way be rough if that is where you will end your struggle and win the race. It is well with your soul.

Nugget No.97 - Your light will grow at dawn, glow brighter at noonday and a luminary at sunset unto a full perfect, fulfilled day

- That is my prayers for you as you go through this book. May your soul find rest and get what you are searching for. Go, grow and glow in your endeavors.

Nugget No.98 - Don't be so heavenly minded that you are of no earthly use nor so earthly minded that you are of no heavenly worth

- The ordeals of the earth should prepare you for heaven and the hope of heaven should lead and guide your ways on earth. Balance your life to fruition.

Nugget No.99 - Leisure time is very necessary and medicinal

- Come unto me all who are heavy laden and I will give you rest, said the Lord. Leisure time is time out, vacation, freedom, rest and taking a walk. All work and no play! If you feel like reading a short sharp historical paranormal fantasy please find my eBook - Angels go to war (Battle for Ehie Dacunga)

Nugget No.100 - May your sky be pure blue, your field ever green, your sea still, your hands richer, your life healthier and your hope heaven worthy.

Nugget No.101 - May your Frightful frustration turn into fortifying fortunes and your impeaching importunity into optimal opportunities

Nugget No.102 - May our stay here on earth be good, your children's world better and your generations.

- May your landmarks never be land mines; your stars never scar nor scares and your efforts never futile

Nugget No.103 - Jesus Christ is the only one worthy of our praise and adoration. No athlete, musician or celebrity died to save you.

- May the mercies of God cloth you, his beauty decorates you, the reason of his Son release you, the gift of the Son lift you, his grace humble you, and his glory crown you. Bon voyage!

APPRECIATION

Thanks for finding time to read this. I hope you have been blessed. I will appreciate if you share this with your friends and write a customer review and rating down the book page online as it will help others share from this blessing too. Thanks so much and may Gods divine favor follow you. Would you like Amazon to notify you by email when I release a new book or the next book in any of the series? Then follow me directly at Amazon. Look for the large yellow Follow button on the left below my photo at this link below and click it. https://amazon.com/author/ikechukwujoseph

Amazon won't give out your email address. God bless you and thanks for visiting. Expect more and bigger blessings

APPENDIX A: ARE YOU BORN AGAIN?

You must be born twice i.e. - the natural or biological birth and the spiritual birth before you can see the kingdom of God. You must be born again. Are you saved? If the Lord comes now will you be taken to heaven? Is your name written in the book of life? Where will you go when you die - heaven or hell? Tell yourself the truth, and do something about your situation. Heaven is a prepared place and for prepared people. Hell is a prepared place and for unprepared people. Do you want to be born again? Then

1. Recognize yourself as a sinner

- For all have sinned and come short of the glory of God - Rom. 3:23.

- You are a sinner by birth for in sin did your mother conceive you- Psalm51:5

- You are a sinner by choice for all we like sheep have gone astray. Isaiah53:6; Rom.6:23.

2. Repent and believe in Jesus Christ

-Repent you therefore, and be converted that you sins may be blotted out, Act 3:19.

3. Confess your sins

-With godly sorrow confess your sins and tell God you are

sorry. Ask him to forgive you all. 1 John.1:9.

4. Accept Jesus Christ into your heart.

Say this Sinner's Prayer - Lord Jesus, I thank you for forgiving me according to your word. Come into my heart. Be my savior and Lord. Remove my name from the book of death and write it in the book of life. By faith I believe I am saved, Amen.

Congratulations for your bold sincere decision and confession. Write me today so that I pray along with you. Join a living church near you where they preach the truth.

APPENDIX B: TESTIMONIES

-Ordinary Men with Extraordinary Power

-Common Men with Uncommon Results

-Usual Men with Unusual Anointing

-Weak Men with Mighty Deeds

-Unschooled Mortal Men with Immortal Visions and PhD-Producing Life Histories

- **Faiths miracle** on wattpad about my book, Discovering Yourself - OMG! This is amazing. You should update more. This is just I don't know extraordinary. May the good Lord bless you. I'm in love already with this book.

- **Misstmaria** on wattpad about my book - Discovering Yourself - Wow!!!! This is incredible and how right you are. What a wonderful lesson here!! Thank you!

- **ByronWalke**r - I really enjoyed the book (Strategic Spiritual Warfare). ByronWalker6 voted on Wattpad for Strategic Spiritual Warfare

- I Love reading although I took my time to read this book it is full of the anointing. Stayed up reading until i could not anymore, already daylight in morning - got some rest and woke up in the presence of God to worship that is how it impacted me.

The prayers in this book also stirred up a desire within me to see the answers to those prayers. I will read more books from this Author

He knows the scripture and speaks clearly and the anointing backs him up all glory to God.

Go ahead read it you'll be glad and you will be touch by the beautiful presence of the Holy Spirit awesome read and will re-read again. Everyone should read this book highly recommended (referring to Holy Spirit Anointing: Bible Faith Nuggets Series Book 5)

-Rebecca Belardo (Georgia) -

- Thank you so much for this book .It just showed up on my Kindle when I was seeking a Word from The Lord . This truth is truly from The Lord THANK YOU SO MUCH. JUANITA. USA

- Rated 5 stars, It was so refreshing - By jamar w jackson

- Loved it. I learned a lot of things in this book. Wow it was Slender. Loved this book PRAISE God

- Five Stars By Gary blakely, Format: Kindle Edition Verified Purchase

Great Book on the anointing, if you want to learn more

- Five Stars by Betty H

Great book, full of wisdom, awesome author/writer!

- By Smackeyon - Power packed and informative.

- Five Stars by Will Pearceon - Very good and enlightening.

- By Amazon Customer "rosa lee watson" rated Five Stars

Love it.

- Greetings am so blessed while searching books on amazon came across your book the Holy Spirit Anointing Bible Faith nuggets book 5. I started reading and truly did not want to stop. Am at page 690 it has really lifted me up and am anticipating to finish reading it and looking to read other books. It has just brought an awakening and ministered to me deeply. Thank you for sharing the knowledge God has grace you with, God bless you Joseph. Attentive and embracing God's presence Prophetess Rebecca

- Merry Christmas Pastor Joseph, you have been a big blessing to me by your messages that I have been receiving. I have used them on my pulpit. God bless you and may he shower his blessings upon you.

Your brother Pastor E. A. [Kenya]

- Dear Pastor Joseph,

You have been of a great blessing to me so much. Your teachings are so encouraging and very powerful. I am praying for you so much. I have been getting your teaching materials and I have been asking myself where you are coming from? Which country? May God bless you so much.

Pastor N. O. O (Kenya).

- Dear pastor IK,

Thanks so much for the inspirational messages you have been sending to me. They have been of a very great help. God will richly bless you.... Pastor Benjam

- My name is Matthew. I received an e-mail that was not intended for me. But i see God's divine hand diverting it to me. It was not even addressed to me at all. it was sent to Veronica Argentina. I have been seeking Gods anointing on the ministry he has called me into. And i have realized before I even received your e-mail that i did not want to do this without Gods hand of anointing upon it. There are just too many people out there that are in ministry that have not been anointed and called with anointing. If I speak or lay hands on someone for healing and do not have Gods hand in it I would rather not even bother. As of late I have been just seeking a deeper relationship with Jesus and only ministering to those that the lord sets right in front of me. The Lord has given me a great burden for the broken heart and the captive to sin; my own heart is broken before the lord in this. When I was in Peru I tasted of this anointing and as i came back to the U.S. there remain a remnant of that anointing for a while. But last night i was asked to speak and it was just words without the power of the life of Christ in them, i have grieved throw the night and woke to find this e-mail that was not even intended for me. (N.B: Bible Faith Nuggets Serous Edition he received was on Davidic Anointing. Same time he was asking for anointing from God). I love the lord so much and want to serve him. He has done so much for me. I will never be able to repay him for his goodness. SEEKING GOD DIRECTION IN MY LIFE AND WHAT HE WANT ME TO DO AND GO.

- G. M (U.S.A)

- AWESOME Book. I'm glad you allow God to speak thru you to tell me where I was off track and how I should now proceed and proceed through this journey. Thank You and may God continue to Bless You.

- D. Woodrow

Hi, Pastor Joe,

I am actually blessed with your newsletter, even though we have not been able to have time together whether physically or on net. Please keep the line hot, for the Lord is your strength.

Shalom.- O.J

Dear Pastor Joseph,

Thanks a lot for your words of inspiration and insight. May God richly bless you and the ministry to continue with the good work you are doing?

P. H

Thanks for your message. I wonder where you got this from. Keep the candle burning.

-E.V (yahoo mails)

Pastor Joseph,

Thanks for all the sweet messages you have been sending. This is to wish you the best of this glorious year. I want to let you know that the Good Lord will continue to bless and uphold you

J. M (Nigerian)

Thank you my brother. You are sent by God. I have started my fasting today and I am very encouraged by these messages. Are you in Africa or abroad?

N.O (South Africa)

I am very much happy to have received this wonderful Book from you. I thank you and I wish to say that there is nothing you could have done better for me then this Book you have sent to me. Oh Pastor just the very few pages I have had the chance to read, I was tempted to say it was just me in the picture. I really am happy to have this Book. I wish you all the best and I say stay blessed but like the little Oliver, I ask for more. Merry Christmas and a Happy New Year!

-D. J. N (GHANA)

Pastor Joseph,

You never, never cease to bless me. I loved the writing on the borrowed axe head! AMEN.AMEN.AMEN!!!!!! (full title of the Edition she referred to was Borrowed Axe-Borrowed Anointing)

-Pastor D. S(U.S.A)

This is truly an eye opening message that came straight from the throne room of God. I passed it on so others may be blessed.

-Evangelist Valrie (U.S.A)

Beloved,

Thanks a million for this and others you've been sending. They've all blessed my heart.

Shalom. U.I (Nigeria)

I am not sure how I managed to get on your mailing list but thanks this was something God wanted me to hear (Referring to Bible Faith Nuggets).

LYN

Hi Pastor,

I was edified after reading this nugget, the almighty God give you more inspiration and knowledge of His word.

-CO.(U.S.A)

Dearly beloved,

Thanks for your beautiful and inspirational messages, they are so timely , may the lord continue to make space for you in this ministry, do please include your contact phone number, I like to speak with you .God bless you real good. Amen .I.E

Greetings Ikechukwu,

Blessings and greetings in Jesus' precious name! Thank you for your letter and words of encouragement! May God use you for the establishment of His Kingdom in the earth, and establish truth and justice. The LORD reigns, let the earth be glad; let the distant shores rejoice. Remain blessed in HIM!

-Pastor S.A (Ukraine)

Dear Joe

Thanks for your love, and also thanks for sending me a good message that bless my soul, i enjoyed it. May the lord richly bless you, thank you so much.

REV. V. U .J (Nigeria)

Dear Pastor, good day in Jesus Name. I read your book but I see it that God want to give me Victory because what I have read so far describes my 11 year old problem.

Kate (Nigeria)

I Praise the Lord for all you that have sent me, emails of encouragement. If I would express how it had made me feel, we would all be in tears.

-Evangelist Neal (U.S.A)

ABOUT THE AUTHOR

Pastor Ikechukwu Joseph is an international consulting educator, publisher, a notable poet, author, speaker and song writer. Ikechukwu Joseph, the author of Discovering Yourself and the publisher of bestselling Unlocking Closed Doors, Strategic Spiritual Warfare, Holy Spirit Anointing, The Study of the Book of Colossians (a verse-by-verse analytical study commentary), A Study of the Book of Philippians (a verse-by-verse analytical study commentary) and many more, trained as a Science Educator, Biologist, System Engineer and Website Developer.

Ikechukwu is the president of the Living Way Ministries and director of The Living Way Productions, The Living Way Academy, a non-profit making organization established under the leading of the Holy Spirit to minister to the body of Christ through conferences, seminars, books, music and end-time deliverance messages. This worldwide outreach of the Living Way Ministries is supported by gifts of those who are interested and concerned with reaching out to the perishing world

Ikechukwu is also a graduate with M. Ed, B. SC and a duly accredited ordained Minister with Evangelistic Messengers Association International, Tennessee, U.S.A. Pastor Joseph served God under different organizations like The Scripture Union, Four Square Gospel Church, NIFES, Fellowship of Christian Students, Grace of God Mission, and Believers Gospel Mission before God led him into the Harvest field.

AUTHOR'S CONTACT

Email:

tlwgom@yahoo.com

Telephone:

+2348035033228

+2348022957255

###

Connect with Me Online

Twitter: http://twitter.com/ikechukwujosep1

Facebook: http://facebook.com/ikechukwu2joseph

www.ingramcontent.com/pod-product-compliance
Lightning Source LLC
Chambersburg PA
CBHW071124240526
45465CB00023B/807